l'âme, la puissance

vous donné

Parmi les plus

faibles, vous

si beaux,

que

sur la

TABLE OF CONTENTS:

Pretty girls   2
To a man leaving for the hunt   8
The child   14
After the battle   23
An old song of younger times   31
On a barricade   40
Oceano nox   46
Pirate's Song   55
Vivar   65
At Dawn, Tomorrow...   74
The Beggar   80
The Word   86
Tonight in clouds the sun has gone to bed...   90

ISBN 1-56163-390-9
© 2002 Petit a Petit
© 2001 The University of Chicago for the translations to The Child, Vivar, Oceano Nox,
Pretty Girls, Tonight in the Clouds..., At Dawn, Tomorrow.... Reproduced by permission.
© 2001, 2002 from Victor Hugo, Selected Poetry by Steven Monte for the translation to The
Beggar. Reproduced by permission of Routledge/Taylor Francis Books, Inc.
© 2004 Joe Johnson for the translations to An Old Song of Younger Times and The Word
© 2004 Beth Droppleman for the translation to To a Man...
© 2004 NBM for the translations of background texts.
Lettering by Ortho
Printed in Singapore

3   2   1

Library of Congress Cataloging-in-Publication Data

Hugo, Victor, 1802-1885.
    [Poemes de Victor Hugo en bandes dessinees. English.]
    The adapted Victor Hugo.
        p. cm. -- (Comics poetry)
    ISBN 1-56163-390-9
        I. Hugo, Victor, 1802-1885--Translations into English. I. Title. II. Series.

PQ2283.P1 2004
841'.7--dc22

2004040240

the adapted
Victor Hugo

Series Editor:
Joe Johnson

Cover:
Timmy Zecevic

Background texts:
Christophe Renault

Design:
Olivier Petit
Cedric Illand

NBM
ComicsLit

Pretty Girls

You write them sonnets (sometimes pretty good);
You kiss the hands they deign to offer to you;
You go with them to church, or through the wood;
You become Damis, and Clitandre, too;

At the balls where they shine, you urge your suit;
You dance and laugh; and while you waltz around
Accompanied by oboe or by lute,
You hear them murmuring this lovely sound:

"Warfare is pious; power is everything;
Knowledge is dangerous; hanging is good;
More jails, and fewer schools, need to be built;

Our forts should be munitioned to the hilt
To stop the plebs from stirring." —These doves would
Set dead-and-buried skeletons shuddering!

July 1870, from Les Quatre
Vents de l'esprit, 1881
Translation by E. H. and A.
M. Blackmore.

Two children are playing in the garden. They are friends because their parents are, too. He is Victor, and she is Adele. They are holding each other's hand and, one day, having grown up, he asks for hers. Their parents are against the marriage, but the sweethearts are stubborn. Wresting parental consent, they get married at the age of twenty.

Their wedding night is splendid, for both are virgins and, flush with youth, they give themselves to one another nine times. A fruitful couple, their love gives birth to five children. Victor is a good husband, but Adele, for her part, grows weary: Sainte-Beuve, a family friend, will become her lover.

Victor escapes from this tragedy into vaudeville. Since he no longer has another half, there's no further question of being monogamous. He cheats on her, and soon more than a little, with Juliette Drouot his lifelong official mistress, with occasional servant women, sweet adventure-seekers, gracious courtesans, and a few pretty women!

5

6

SET DEAD-
AND-BURIED
SKELETONS
SHUDDERING!

To a man leaving for the hunt

Yes, Man's answerable, a reckoning faces.

On earth, where dawn each turning day darkness chases,

Be a steward of God, but an honest steward.

Quake at every abuse of power by beast endured.

Do you believe yourself of such crowning finish

That you may fearlessly become oh so hellish,

Voracious, sensual, voluptuous, ferocious,

The ass driven to death, the nag worn unconscious,

You fatten up the finch by putting out its eyes,

And, each year, slaughter the woods three, four times besides?

This happy hunter his gun or trap loading,

Verges on murder and sacrilege approaching.

Thinking is your purpose; surviving is your right.

Killing for sport is not. Do you believe aright

The sun to the nettle a silky brush attached,

The blackberry painted, or the sorb's fruit ripened

So a tastier roasted quail you might assay?

God who creates birds makes them not so you may prey.

from Dernière Gerbe,
Oeuvre posthume, 1902
Translation by Beth Droppleman.

The famous literary critic Sainte-Beuve is on the hunt right from entering the Hugos' home. Clumsy and sickly, from his youngest years he was taunted by his peers. They nicknamed him "Tomcat." It was apt chosen, too, for while the man longs for a pen, he will only find claws! He also has a knack for stroking Hugo's ego. He insinuates himself into the Hugo household. He admires the master's eloquence and is ever so sensi the wife's beauty. He prey on to them. When the couple moves to 11, rue Notre-Dame-des-Champs, takes up at number 19. res to show his verses who gives him advice and to address sweet smiles to the mincing wife. She falls prey to him! Hugo learns of it and soon has his vengeance: it falls to him to welcome Sainte-Beuve into the Académie Française. Will he destroy Sainte-Beuve? He merely gives a just estimation. Our author has a lion's nobility: he does not deign to bag that poor, slinking puss.

ON EARTH, WHERE DAWN EACH TURNING DAY DARKNESS CHASES,

YES, MAN'S ANSWERABLE, A RECKONING FACES.

BE A STEWARD OF GOD, BUT AN HONEST STEWARD.

QUAKE AT EVERY ABUSE OF POWER BY BEAST ENDURED.

The Child

The Turks have been. Destruction everywhere.
Chios, the isle of vines, lies black and bare—
Chios, in the leaves' shade,
Whose seas used to reflect its wooded height,
The girls who dances and played.

Deserted. No: beside the blackened stone
A blue-eyed child, a Greek child, sits alone,
And bows his downcast head.
His only stronghold and security
Is a white hawthorn—a bloom equally
Ignored among the dead.

Poor boy, barefooted on such crags and tors!
To wipe the tears from those clear eyes of yours
Hued like the sea and sky,
So that their blue, stormy with weeping, may
Be lit with lightning-shafts of joy and play,
To lift your fair head high,

What do you want? What must we give you, child,
To tie and tidy pleasantly those wild
Ringlets of hair that billow
About you, never shamed by steel—that shed
Themselves in tears over your lovely head
Like the leaves on a willow?

What could relieve you, lad, from all your woes?
The lily, blue as your blue eyes, that grows
By dark pools in Iran?
Or the fruit of the Tuba, that huge tree
Whose shade a horse, galloping constantly,
Takes centuries to span?

Or might a lovely woodbird make you smile—
Singing like neys, but in a sweeter style,
Or like cymbals but louder?
Flower, fruit, or wondrous bird—which is for you?
"My friend," says the Greek boy with eyes of blue,
"I want bullets and powder."

from Les Orientales, 1829
Translation by E. H. and
A. M. Blackmore.

Sophie Trébuchet is a royalist, whereas Léopold Hugo is a general for Napoleon. Everything opposes them, yet they love one another. She scorns the Empire but, ruled by that of her senses, agrees to legitimate their liaison through marriage.

War soon breaks out between the two. The survivors are three boys: Abel, Eugène, and Victor, who, in the thick of the battle, see their parents separate. They go from one home to the other, but finally to their father's, along with their mother, once he becomes the governor of an Italian province.

Their situation is simply too good: Sophie would not disdain it because of the Empire, and her children live like kings, in a palace with a view over a courtyard where a cavalry company is at their father's orders. Thus did a royalist lead her children to make a secret hero of an officer of Napoleon.

THE TURKS HAVE BEEN.
DESTRUCTION EVERYWHERE.
CHIOS, THE ISLE OF VINES, LIES
BLACK AND BARE

CHIOS, IN THE LEAVES' SHADE,

WHOSE SEAS USED TO
REFLECT ITS WOODED HEIGHT,
ITS SLOPES AND VILLAS, AND
SOMETIMES AT NIGHT

THE GIRLS WHO DANCES AND PLAYED.

DESERTED. NO: BESIDE THE BLACKENED STONE A BLUE-EYED CHILD, A GREEK CHILD, SITS ALONE,

AND BOWS HIS DOWNCAST HEAD.

HIS ONLY STRONGHOLD AND SECURITY IS A WHITE HAWTHORN- A BLOOM EQUALLY

IGNORED AMONG THE DEAD.

POOR BOY, BAREFOOTED ON
SUCH CRAGS AND TORS!
TO WIPE THE TEARS FROM
THOSE CLEAR EYES OF YOURS

HUED LIKE THE SEA AND SKY,

SO THAT THEIR BLUE,
STORMY WITH WEEPING, MAY
BE LIT WITH LIGHTNING-SHAFTS
OF JOY AND PLAY,

TO LIFT YOUR FAIR HEAD HIGH,

5

18

WHAT DO YOU WANT? WHAT MUST WE GIVE YOU, CHILD, TO TIE AND TIDY PLEASANTLY THOSE WILD

RINGLETS OF HAIR THAT BILLOW

ABOUT YOU, NEVER SHAMED BY STEEL—THAT SHED THEMSELVES IN TEARS OVER YOUR LOVELY HEAD

LIKE THE LEAVES ON A WILLOW?

BY DARK POOLS IN IRAN?

OR THE FRUIT OF THE TUBA, THAT HUGE TREE WHOSE SHADE A HORSE, GALLOPING CONSTANTLY,

TAKES CENTURIES TO SPAN?

WHAT COULD RELIEVE YOU, LAD, FROM ALL YOUR WOES? THE LILY, BLUE AS YOUR BLUE EYES, THAT GROWS

5

OR MIGHT A LOVELY WOODBIRD MAKE YOU SMILE-

SINGING LIKE NEYS, BUT IN A SWEETER STYLE,

OR LIKE CYMBALS BUT LOUDER?

FLOWER, FRUIT, OR WONDROUS BIRD-WHICH IS FOR YOU?

"MY FRIEND," SAYS THE GREEK BOY WITH EYES OF BLUE,

I WANT BULLETS AND POWDER!!

After the battle

My father, hero of benignant mien,
On horseback visited the gory scene,
After the battle as the evening fell,
And took with him a trooper loved right well,
Because of bravery and presence bold.
The field was covered with the dead, all cold,
And shades of night were deepening. Came a sound
Feeble and hoarse, from something on the ground;
It was a Spaniard of the vanquished force,
Who dragged himself with pain beside their course;
Wounded and bleeding, livid and half dead,
"Give me to drink—in pity, drink!" he said.
My father, touched, stretched to his follower now,
A flask of rum that from his saddle-bow
Hung down. "The poor soul—give him drink," said he.
But while the trooper prompt, obediently
Stooped towards the other, he of Moorish race
Pointed a pistol at my father's face,
And with a savage oath the trigger drew;
The hat flew off, a bullet passing through.
As swerved his charger in a backward stride,
"Give him to drink the same," my father cried.

Victor Hugo, from La Légende
des siècles, book 3, 1883
Translation by Mrs. Newton
Crosland in H. L. Williams.

Victor Hugo is not one of those men who, aging after the battle, lose their ideals along with their hair. Quite the contrary, it is while aging that he acts the young man. Though risking the loss of his wealth, he stands up against evil. Though risking the loss of his life, he refuses to play dead, calls out the ruling class, and sides with one group alone: the oppressed.

He clamors for the equality of the sexes, denounces capital punishment, waxes indignant against wars, and affirms the rights of children. When threatened, he exiles himself. Paying in body and with his own means, he devotes a third of his expenditures to the most destitute.

For eight years in Guernsey, he has a daily meal served to impoverished children and, every December 25th, throws them a party with toys. He who had been a royalist has become a republican. In the winter of his life, his hair whitening under the years, he remembers his father in order to play Father Christmas.

MY FATHER, HERO OF BENIGNANT MIEN, ON HORSEBACK

THE HAT FLEW OFF, A BULLET PASSING THROUGH.

AS SWERVED HIS CHARGER IN A BACKWARD STRIDE,

"GIVE HIM TO
DRINK THE SAME,"
MY FATHER CRIED.

An old song of younger times

I had never dreamt of Rose;
To the woods Rose with me came;
We were talking I suppose
But of what I cannot claim.

As cold, I was, as marble;
With distracted steps I walked;
Of flowers, trees I'd babble,
"And?" her eyes, it seemed, did talk.

Morning dew its pearls displayed,
The thicket its parasols;
I went and heard the blackbirds,
And Rose the nightingale's calls.

Me, sixteen, seeming morose;
Her, twenty, with shining eyes.
The nightingales warbled Rose
While blackbirds me, scornful cries.

Rose, standing straight on haunches,
Her trembling arm raised with charm,
Berries to take from branches.
I didn't see her white arm.

Adaptation : *Daniel Pecqueur* - Art : *Eric Nosal*

Over velvety mosses,
A cool stream in hollow flowed;
And an amorous Nature
In great, unhearing groves dozed.

Her shoe did Rose remove,
With ingenuous air did put
Dainty foot in water pure.
I didn't see her bare foot.

I knew not what to tell her;
Followed her through grove did I,
Seeing her sometimes smiling
And more than once softly sigh.

Her beauty I didn't see
Till gone from unhearing groves.
"Okay! We'll forget it," said she.
Ever since, my mind there roves.

from Les Contemplations,
book 1, poem 19, 1856
Translation by Joe Johnson.

Victor Hugo was born in Besançon on February 26, 1802. He is so puny, they do not think he will survive very long. He does so, however, and, at the age of six-teen months, is weighed down with a head so enor-mous that people think him a dwarf and almost certain-ly "weak-minded."

Having started his child-hood in such a fashion, Hugo might have had an aversion for that period. On the contrary, he clings to a profound nostalgia. Ah! that Miss Rose, the teach-er's daughter at his first school, whom he'd watch while she'd put on her hose. And that house, at the Impasse des Feuillantines where, from ages seven to ten he used to love tussling with his brothers and play-ing with Adèle Fouche, the little brunette who would become his wife.

He remembers the bloom one has as a child and the sense of fantasy, which he puts into his poems. Old songs of younger days taken up anew, after his death by great singers like Brassens, Reggiani, and Montand.

I HAD NEVER DREAMT OF ROSE; TO THE WOODS ROSE WITH ME CAME;

WE WERE TALKING I SUPPOSE BUT OF WHAT I CANNOT CLAIM.

AS COLD, I WAS, AS MARBLE;
WITH DISTRACTED STEPS I
WALKED; OF FLOWERS,
TREES I'D BABBLE,

"AND?" HER EYES, IT
SEEMED, DID TALK.

MORNING DEW ITS
PEARLS DISPLAYED, THE
THICKET ITS PARASOLS;

I WENT AND HEARD THE BLACKBIRDS, AND ROSE THE NIGHTINGALE'S CALLS.

ME, SIXTEEN, SEEMING MOROSE; HER, TWENTY, WITH SHINING EYES.

THE NIGHTINGALES WARBLED ROSE WHILE BLACKBIRDS ME, SCORNFUL CRIES.

ROSE, STANDING STRAIGHT ON HAUNCHES, HER TREMBLING ARM RAISED WITH CHARM,

BERRIES TO TAKE FROM BRANCHES. I DIDN'T SEE HER WHITE ARM.

OVER VELVETY MOSSES, A COOL STREAM IN HOLLOW FLOWED;

AND AN AMOROUS NATURE IN GREAT, UNHEARING GROVES DOZED.

HER SHOE DID ROSE REMOVE, WITH INGENUOUS AIR DID PUT

DAINTY FOOT IN WATER PURE. I DIDN'T SEE HER BARE FOOT.

EVER SINCE, MY MIND
THERE ROVES.

On a barricade

Upon a barricade thrown 'cross the street
Where patriot's blood with felon's stains one's feet,
Ta'en with grown men, a lad aged twelve, or less!
"Were you among them—you?" He answered: "Yes."
"Good," said the officer, "when comes your turn,
You'll be shot, too." —The lad sees lightnings burn,—
Stretched 'neath the wall his comrades one by one:
Then says to the officer, "First let me run
And take this watch home to my mother, sir?"
"You want to escape?" —"No, I'll come back."—"What fear
These brats have! Where do you live?" —"By the well, below.
I'll return quickly if you let me go."
"Be off, young scamp!" Off went the boy. "Good joke!"
And here from all a hearty laugh outbroke,
And with this laugh the dying mixed their moan.
But the laugh suddenly ceased, when, paler grown,
'Midst them the lad appeared, and breathlessly
Stood upright 'gainst the wall with: "Here am I."

Dull death was ashamed; the officer said, "Be free!"

From L'Année Terrible, 1872
Translation by N. R. T. in H. L. Williams.

Parisians have two failings: cannons and Republican ideals. Where did they get those mortars? They bought their own armaments from public collections! What will they do with their ideals? An uprising to overthrow the National Assembly. Elected the latter as its chief executive, Adolphe Thiers frets accordingly. On March 18, 1871, he sends in his troops to confiscate the Parisians' cannons. This sets off the powder keg. The insurgents shoot a general. He is the first victim of a revolutionary movement called the Commune. Thiers orders his soldier to fire. People fall on the barricades. More than 25,000 Parisians are massacred. This makes Hugo's blood boil: "I accuse misery! Let's make the downtrodden treasure life; that's the only way to prevent revolutions. You have no right to assassinate people as you're doing, the majority of whom rose up out of dignity and are then crushed.

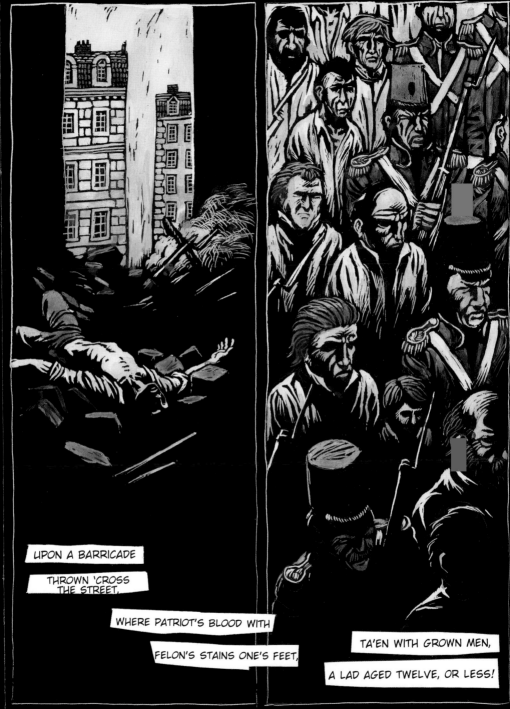

UPON A BARRICADE

THROWN 'CROSS THE STREET,

WHERE PATRIOT'S BLOOD WITH FELON'S STAINS ONE'S FEET,

TA'EN WITH GROWN MEN, A LAD AGED TWELVE, OR LESS!

-"WERE YOU AMONG THEM-YOU?"

HE ANSWERED: "YES."

"GOOD," SAID THE OFFICER,

"WHEN COMES YOUR TURN,

YOU'LL BE SHOT, TOO."

THE LAD SEES LIGHTNINGS BURN,

STRETCHED 'NEATH THE WALL

HIS COMRADES ONE BY ONE:

THEN SAYS TO THE OFFICER,

"FIRST LET ME RUN

AND TAKE THIS WATCH

HOME TO MY MOTHER, SIR?"

"YOU WANT TO ESCAPE?"- "NO, I'LL

COME BACK."- "WHAT FEAR
THESE BRATS HAVE!

WHERE DO YOU LIVE?"- "BY THE WELL,

BELOW: I'LL RETURN QUICKLY

IF YOU LET ME GO."

"BE OFF, YOUNG SCAMP!" OFF WENT THE BOY.

"GOOD JOKE!"

AND HERE FROM ALL A

HEARTY LAUGH OUTBROKE,

AND WITH THIS LAUGH THE

DYING MIXED THEIR MOAN.

BUT THE LAUGH
SUDDENLY

CEASED, WHEN, PALER GROWN,

'MIDST THEM THE LAD

APPEARED, AND
BREATHLESSLY

STOOD UPRIGHT 'GAINST THE WALL WITH:

Oceano Nox

How many captains and their sailors went
Blithely toward some distant continent
Beyond this bleak horizon, and were lost!
How many vanished-a cruel destiny!-
One moonless night in some unfathomed sea,
In whose blind depths forever they are tossed!

How many skippers perished with their crew!
Across the surge some blast of tempest blew,
And their lives' pages all were scattered then.
Plunged in the chasm-who will know their fate?
Each passing wave seized some part of the freight,
And this one took the skiff, and that the men.

No one can tell their doom, the poor lost heads
Rolling across those somber ocean beds,
Beating their dead brows in the unknown black.
How many parents, with one dream left, died
Awaiting daily at the harbor's side
   Those who did not come back!

At night people talk of you sometimes here,
Sitting in joyous groups on rusty gear;
Still, now and then, your shadowy names succeed
The songs and laughs and tales of foreign tides
And kisses stolen from your promised brides
While you are sleeping in the salt green weed.

"Why has so-and-so left us all this while?
Could he be king in some more prosperous isle?"
But then your memory vanishes away.
Bodies decay in seas, and names in minds.
Time adds to shadows shades of darker kinds:
Somber oblivion blends with somber spray.

Soon, from the eyes of all, your shade has passed.
One has a plow to tend, and one a mast.
Only, at night, when conquering tempests roll,
Your white-browed widows, weary with their waiting,
Still name you, stirring ash within the grating
            Of their hearth and their soul.

And when the grave has shut their eyelids too,
Not even a stone remains to speak of you
Within the narrow echoing cemetery,
Not even a willow dropping foliage,
Not even a beggar on some ancient bridge
Singing a drab and simple melody.

Where are the sailors swallowed by dark seas?
Waves feared by every mother on her knees,
Deep waves, what dreadful tales you could recite!
You tell them to us when you climb our shores,
And that is why you utter such wild roars
When you are coming to our verge at night.

Victor Hugo
(Les rayons et les ombres - 1840)
Translation by E.H. and A.M. Blackmore

Victor Hugo is always fascinated by waves. On July 16, 1836, he witnesses a hurricane's wrath on the cliffs at Saint-Valér[...] Somme. He does not delay in writing down his impressions of the day by borrowing from Virgil a phrase that he makes into a title: "Ruit oceano nox," which means "Night collapses over the Ocean." Later, at Guernsey, he has a glass solarium built atop his house, which becomes his study. He works with his eyes cast over the sea.

From his contemplation of waves, he brings forth worlds. The wind churns the waves in the same way as he loves to move tables and conduct seances. H[...] on a quest for the dead and, when the night carries them away from the sea, he goes in search of them around a table: he calls forth spirits. When the water below is no longer visible, there remains to him the beyond, from where his eldest daughter answers him to soothe his wavering soul.

OCÉANO NOX

HOW MANY CAPTAINS AND THEIR SAILORS WENT BLITHELY TOWARD SOME DISTANT CONTINENT

BEYOND THIS BLEAK HORIZON, AND WERE LOST!

HOW MANY VANISHED— A CRUEL DESTINY!— ONE MOONLESS NIGHT IN SOME UNFATHOMED SEA,

IN WHOSE BLIND DEPTHS FOREVER THEY ARE TOSSED!

1

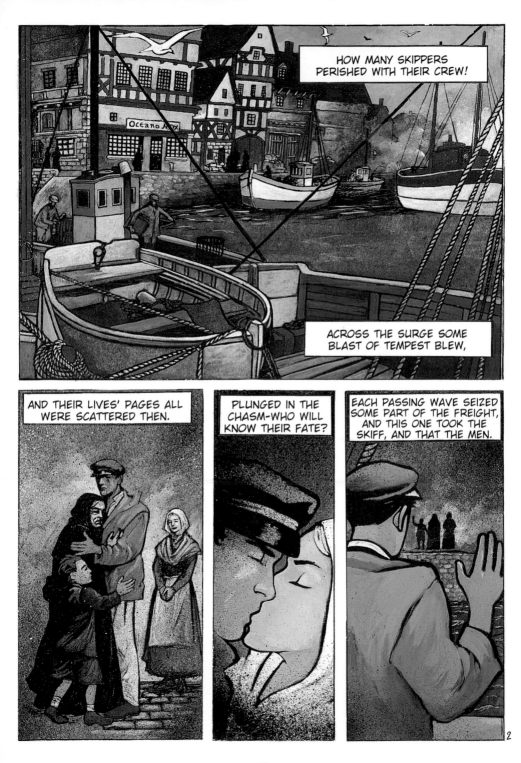

HOW MANY SKIPPERS PERISHED WITH THEIR CREW!

ACROSS THE SURGE SOME BLAST OF TEMPEST BLEW,

AND THEIR LIVES' PAGES ALL WERE SCATTERED THEN.

PLUNGED IN THE CHASM-WHO WILL KNOW THEIR FATE?

EACH PASSING WAVE SEIZED SOME PART OF THE FREIGHT, AND THIS ONE TOOK THE SKIFF, AND THAT THE MEN.

NO ONE CAN TELL
THEIR DOOM, THE
POOR LOST HEADS

ROLLING ACROSS THOSE
SOMBER OCEAN BEDS,

BEATING THEIR DEAD BROWS
IN THE UNKNOWN BLACK.

HOW MANY PARENTS,
WITH ONE DREAM LEFT,
DIED AWAITING DAILY
AT THE HARBOR'S SIDE

THOSE WHO DID
NOT COME BACK!

"WHY HAS SO-AND-SO LEFT US ALL THIS WHILE?

COULD HE BE KING IN SOME MORE PROSPEROUS ISLE?"

BUT THEN YOUR MEMORY VANISHES AWAY.

BODIES DECAY IN SEAS, AND NAMES IN MINDS. TIME ADDS TO SHADOWS SHADES OF DARKER KINDS:

SOMBER OBLIVION BLENDS WITH SOMBER SPRAY.

5

SOON, FROM THE EYES OF ALL,
YOUR SHADE HAS PASSED.
ONE HAS A PLOW TO TEND, AND ONE A MAST.

ONLY, AT NIGHT, WHEN
CONQUERING TEMPESTS ROLL,

YOUR WHITE-BROWED WIDOWS,
WEARY WITH THEIR WAITING,
STILL NAME YOU, STIRRING
ASH WITHIN THE GRATING,

OF THEIR HEARTH
AND THEIR SOUL.

Rosanna
Calec
1918 — 1998

AND WHEN THE GRAVE HAS SHUT THEIR EYELIDS TOO,
NOT EVEN A STONE REMAINS TO SPEAK OF YOU
WITHIN THE NARROW ECHOING CEMETERY,
NOT EVEN A WILLOW DROPPING FOLIAGE,
NOT EVEN A BEGGAR ON SOME ANCIENT BRIDGE
SINGING A DRAB AND SIMPLE MELODY.

Pirate's Song

We're bearing five-score Christian dogs
  To serve the cruel drivers:
Some are fair beauties gently born,
  And some rough coral-divers.
We hardy skimmers of the sea
  Are lucky in each sally,
And, eighty strong, we send along,
  The dreaded Pirate Galley.

A nunnery was spied ashore,
  We lowered away the cutter,
And, landing, seized the youngest nun
  Ere she a cry could utter;
Beside the creek, deaf to our oars,
  She slumbered in green alley,
As, eighty strong, we sent along,
  The dreaded Pirate Galley.

"Be silent, darling, you must come—
  The wind is off shore blowing;
You only change your prison dull
  For one that's splendid, glowing!
His Highness dotes on milky cheeks,
  So do not make us dally"—
We, eighty strong, who send along,
  The dreaded Pirate Galley.

She sought to flee back to her cell,
  And called us each a devil!
"You'd dare?"—"We would," the chief did tell.
  She weeps, forlorn, dishevel;
But, spite of buffet, prayers, and calls,
  Too late her friends to rally—
We, eighty strong, bore her along
  Unto the Pirate Galley.

The fairer for her tears profuse
  As dews refresh the flower,
She is well worth three purses full,
  And will adorn the bower—
For vain her vow: "I'll pine and die!"
  Thus torn from her dear valley·
She reigns, and we still row along
  The dreaded Pirate Galley.

from Les Orientales, 1829
Translation by Henry Llewellyn Williams.

Victor Hugo, a great name in literature, answers to the nickname "Toto" when he is with Juliette Drouet. He has fun with it; he's like a child! The eminent writer adores fantasy, willingly slipping into his most somber works silly songs, plays on words, rhymes, and rhythms, loving puns and nonsense: "My dinner harasses and addles: while eating horse, I think of saddles." In Ruy Blas, he creates a character who expresses his mockery, Don César, a companion of bandits, a blustering picaro, who, amongst all his rejoinders, has one bravura bit, when, upon arriving via a chimney to set the stage afire: "When I'm in a good fight, I don't let go." Could be said today! That "Toto" is a real pirate! He scuttles the old Classics and, although it leads to the spilling of lots of ink, opens new horizons for the stage.

WE'RE BEARING FIVE-SCORE CHRISTIAN DOGS TO SERVE THE CRUEL DRIVERS:

SOME ARE FAIR BEAUTIES GENTLY BORN,

AND SOME ROUGH CORAL-DIVERS.

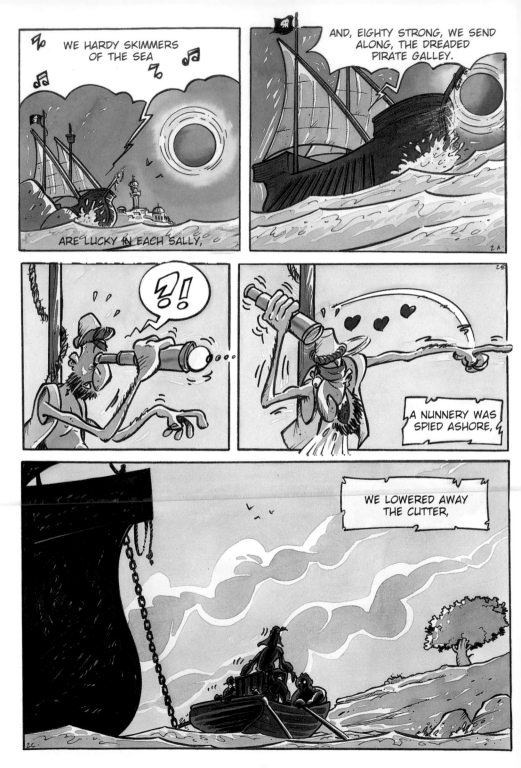

59

BE SILENT, DARLING, YOU MUST COME- THE WIND IS OFF SHORE BLOWING;

YOU ONLY CHANGE YOUR PRISON DULL FOR ONE THAT'S SPLENDID, GLOWING!

HIS HIGHNESS DOTES ON MILKY CHEEKS, SO DO NOT MAKE US DALLY"-

WE, EIGHTY STRONG,

WHO SEND ALONG, THE DREADED PIRATE GALLEY.

AND CALLED US EACH A DEVIL! "YOU'D DARE?"

"WE WOULD,"

THE CHIEF DID TELL.

SHE WEEPS, FORLORN, DISHEVEL; BUT, SPITE OF BUFFET, PRAYERS, AND CALLS,

SNIF! SNIF!

SHE SOUGHT TO FLEE BACK TO HER CELL,

?

?!

SNIF! SNIF!

TOO LATE HER FRIENDS TO RALLY-

SHE IS WELL WORTH THREE PURSES FULL,

AND WILL ADORN THE BOWER—

FOR VAIN HER VOW

"I'LL PINE AND DIE!"

THUS TORN FROM HER DEAR VALLEY;

SHE REIGNS,

63

Vivar

Vivar, a very dark old manor, turreted
And square, lay in the depths of a wood; the courtyard
Was small, the gate was ugly. When Sheik Yahia
(Later, King of Toledo) visited
The Cid on his return from Cintra,
The Moorish Prince entered the narrow patio.
A man with currycomb in hand was grooming
A filly tethered to the railings;
The sheik could only see his back; the man
Had just spread out some burdens on the ground—
Manger, sack of oats, harness, saddle;
On the keep flew Don Diego's banner
(The Cid's father was still alive then); and the man,
Without seeing the sheik, scrubbed, brushed, washed, worked,
Bare-headed, bare-armed, clad in rustic leather.
The sheik said, without even a *buenos días*,
"I have come, fellow, to see the great Campeador
of Castille—Lord Ruy Díaz." And the man,
Turning, replied, "I am he."

"What!" cried Yahia,
"You—the famed hero, valiant Lord of Shields—
I find you thus! Why, if you took the field
And said: 'To arms!' the whole of Spain, from Avis
To Cadafal, from Algarva to Gibraltar,

Would hear the trumpet-blast; above your tent
A host of singing victories winged with wind
Would speed you on your way! Last year, when I
Saw you in the king's palace—I
Prisoner, and you victorious—you seemed
Indeed the regal conqueror of the Ebro;
You had the famous Tizona in your hand;
Your splendor filled the courtyard, as is fitting
For one who is the sunrise; you were truly
A most majestic baron; easier
To pluck straws from a blaze, than to find anyone
Before whose steps you would have given way!
More than one of the grandees took pride
That they were of the Cid's service and retinue;
You came and went and spoke in glory—made
Everyone drink that, just as babes drink milk;
Proud dukes bloated with luxury and bile,
Who, ever since their heads could wear a hat,
Never deferred to any creature living,
Rose up instinctively when you went by.
The gentlemen all served the Cid—he has
His majordomos, like a sovereign; Lerma
And Guzman were your squire and bodyguard;
Your clothes were woven of splendor, and you wore
The majesty of steel, for all your goodness;
Your honey seemed gold-shrouded, like an orange.
Twenty couriers, constantly at the ready,

Tended you. No one was before the Cid,

No one beside him; no one—even royalty,

Infant or Prince—dared to call you his comrade!

Your glory lit the skies with a supremacy

Dazzling to see; wherever you went, whole

Platoons went with you; no peak was too high for you;

You were a figure of such loftiness

The very eagles flew to you. Apart

From military command, you treated all things

As utter worthlessness and vapor; you

Disdained all names except the name of general;

The Cid was supreme magisterial baron.

You dominated all—great, lordless, yokeless,

Absolute, spear in hand, and plume on brow."

"Then," said Rodrigo, "I was merely with the king."

"Why!" cried the sheik, "today, Cid, what has happened?

What garb is this? I come here, and I find you

Dressed like a page, outdoors, bare-armed, bare-headed,

And such a little boy that you are handling

Manger and cavesson with your very hands

To do chores that are fitting for a squire!"

"Sheik," said the Cid, "now I am with my father."

From La Légende des
Siècles, book 1, 1859
Translation by E. H. and
A. M. Blackmore.

When he is nine years old, Victor Hugo rejoins his father and discovers Spain. Immediately taken with its charm, he returns from there haunted by ghosts whom he would later name: Don César, Dona Sol, Ruy Diaz. He is particularly touched by one of the first villages he comes upon: Ernani. He will give its name to his famous play by adding on a fearsome, war-like "H". For that is exactly what he is waging by penning his play: Hernani is explosive, aimed at demolishing classical conventions. And when the play is performed, a battle does take place in the theater where the young romantics oppose the old conservatives. Some boo, while others applaud. Some hurl insults, and others throw them back. When an old bourgeois woman dares to utter mockeries, she immediately hears: "You're wrong to be laughing, lady, 'cause people can see your teeth!" Hernani, having created a scandal, ends up being a success! Victor Hugo is rich, thanks to the stag

VIVAR, A VERY DARK OLD MANOR, TURRETED
AND SQUARE, LAY IN THE DEPTHS OF A WOOD;

WHEN SHEIK YAHIA (LATER, KING OF TOLEDO) VISITED
THE CID ON HIS RETURN FROM CINTRA,

THE COURTYARD WAS
SMALL, THE GATE
WAS UGLY.

THE MOORISH PRINCE ENTERED THE NARROW PATIO.

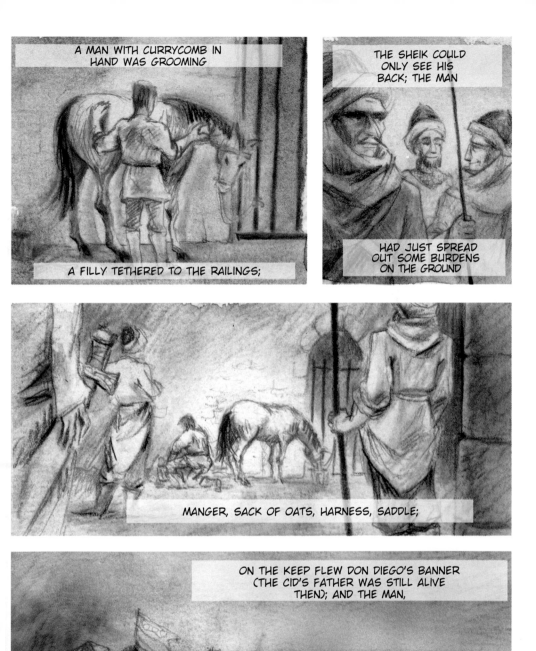

A MAN WITH CURRYCOMB IN HAND WAS GROOMING

A FILLY TETHERED TO THE RAILINGS;

THE SHEIK COULD ONLY SEE HIS BACK; THE MAN

HAD JUST SPREAD OUT SOME BURDENS ON THE GROUND

MANGER, SACK OF OATS, HARNESS, SADDLE;

ON THE KEEP FLEW DON DIEGO'S BANNER (THE CID'S FATHER WAS STILL ALIVE THEN); AND THE MAN,

WITHOUT SEEING THE SHEIK, SCRUBBED,

BRUSHED,

WASHED,

WORKED, BARE-HEADED, BARE-ARMED,

CLAD IN RUSTIC LEATHER.

THE SHEIK SAID, WITHOUT EVEN A *BUENOS DIAS*,

"I HAVE COME, FELLOW, TO SEE THE GREAT CAMPEADOR OF CASTILLE-LORD RUY DIAZ."

AND THE MAN, TURNING, REPLIED:

"I AM HE."

"WHAT!"

"YOU—THE FAMED HERO,

VALIANT

LORD OF SHIELDS

I FIND YOU THUS!

WHY, IF YOU TOOK THE FIELD

AND SAID: 'TO ARMS!' THE WHOLE OF SPAIN, FROM AVUS TO CADAFAL, FROM ALGARVA TO GIBRALTAR, WOULD HEAR THE TRUMPET-BLAST; ABOVE YOUR TENT

A HOST OF SINGING VICTORIES WINGED WITH WIND

WOULD SPEED YOU ON YOUR WAY!

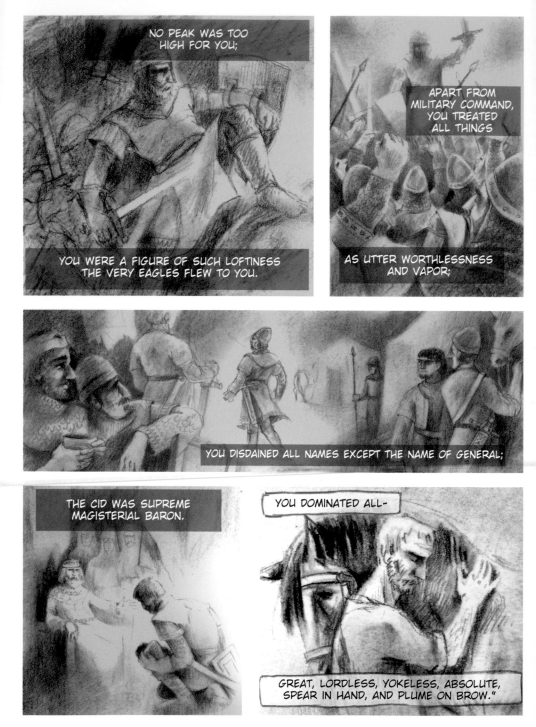

"THEN, I WAS MERELY WITH THE KING."

"WHY! TODAY, CID, WHAT HAS HAPPENED? WHAT GARB IS THIS? I COME HERE, AND I FIND YOU DRESSED LIKE A PAGE, OUTDOORS, BARE-ARMED, BARE-HEADED, AND SUCH A LITTLE BOY THAT YOU ARE HANDLING

MANGER AND CAVESSON WITH YOUR VERY HANDS TO DO CHORES THAT ARE FITTING FOR A SQUIRE!"

"SHEIK,"

"NOW I AM WITH MY FATHER."

At dawn tomorrow...

At dawn tomorrow, when the plains grow bright,
I'll go. You wait for me: I know you do.
I'll cross the woods, I'll cross the mountain-height.
No longer can I keep away from you.

I'll walk along with eyes fixed on my mind-
The world around I'll neither hear nor see-
Alone, unknown, hands crossed, and back inclined;
And day and night will be alike to me.

I'll see neither the gold of evening gloom
Nor the sails off to Harfleur far away;
And when I come, I'll place upon your tomb
Some flowering heather and a holly spray.

from Les Contemplations,
book 4 - poem 14
Translation by E.H. and
A.M. Blackmore

"Victor," a first name worthy of conquerors and "Hugo," two syllables forcing one forward.

Victor Hugo, a man necessarily larger than life! And January 1843 is but a reminder of it, for the year appears to be off to a great start. At the age of forty-one, the famous authors play Les Burgraves *is set to be staged, his eldest daughter will marry, and he will be leaving for Spain with his mistress Juliette Drouet. Theater rehearsals take place, Léopoldine becomes Madame Vacquerie and Juliette packs the bags. His happiness knows no bounds, and is increased by the news that "Didine" is pregnant. But suddenly everything goes wrong. Les Burgraves is booed and, returning from his trip, Hugo learns from the newspapers that his daughter and son-in-law are dead after drowning in a canoe trip at Villequier. His career on stage is floundering, while his daughter dies in the Seine. Feeling at his lowest, Hugo pulls the curtain. He wants to devote himself to verse. He'll write hundreds in his daughter's memory.*

I'LL WALK ALONG WITH EYES FIXED ON MY MIND—

THE WORLD AROUND I'LL NEITHER HEAR NOR SEE— ALONE, UNKNOWN, HANDS CROSSED, AND BACK INCLINED;

AND DAY AND NIGHT WILL BE ALIKE TO ME.

3.

The Beggar

A poor man passed by in the wind and the frost.

I rapped on my window; he stopped and looked lost

In front of the door I opened, then turned around.

The mules were coming back from the market in town,

With peasants on their saddles and bought goods in tow.

The man, I knew, lived in that hut just below

The hill, and ageing, dreamed of things that had the worth

Of sun from sad heavens, or pennies from the earth-

He joined his hands for God and opened them for men.

I shouted: 'Come in here and warm yourself my friend.'

'What's your name?' I asked him. He answered, 'There are some

Who call me the poor one.' I said: 'Enter, *brave homme*.'8

I made him take a bowl of hot milk and some tea.

The man was shivering with cold; he talked to me

And I answered back without listening to him.

'Your clothes are drenched,' I said, 'you should really spread them

In front of the chimney.' He went up to the fire.

His coat, completely eaten by worms, was like wire

A blue cloth now faded, which-pinpricked with holes

Suddenly appearing in the light of the coals-

Covered the hearth, resembling a starry sky.

The moment he spread his tattered coat out to dry

From which I saw puddle water drip here and there,

I thought to myself, 'Ths man is full of prayer,'

And stared, deaf to words and lost in meditations,

At his sackcloth in which I saw constellations.

from *Les Contemplations, 1856*
Translation by Steven Monte.

Suddenly, being in the Académie Française no longer suffices for Hugo: he wants to be a Peer of France. He becomes one. Nowadays, he would be a representative of an M.P. The honor goes to his head. He begins dressing like a dandy and gets his hair curled, frequents salons, and goes from the house of representatives to whorehouses, arising in the former, going to bed in the others. The writer is resting so comfortably he almost seems to be falling asleep.

But soon he is obliged to go into exile. His fortune and his collapse within him. Penniless in Brussels he lives on bread. He makes it to Jersey, then sets up home on Guernsey. There remains but one solution: work! He gives in to expressing his humanity first in the poem cycle Les Contemplations and, in 1862, Les Misérables, which he finally completes after having meditated on it for more than twenty years. Henceforth, Hugo's beard is white; the dandy with curls is good and dead!

A POOR MAN PASSED BY IN THE WIND AND THE FROST.

I RAPPED ON MY WINDOW; HE STOPPED AND LOOKED LOST

IN FRONT OF THE DOOR I OPENED, THEN TURNED AROUND.
THE MULES WERE COMING BACK FROM THE MARKET IN TOWN,
WITH PEASANTS ON THEIR SADDLES AND BOUGHT GOODS IN TOW.

HE WENT UP TO THE FIRE.

HIS COAT, COMPLETELY EATEN BY WORMS, WAS LIKE WIRE,
A BLUE CLOTH NOW FADED, WHICH -PINPRICKED WITH HOLES,

SUDDENLY APPEARING IN THE LIGHT OF
THE COALS- COVERED THE HEARTH,

RESEMBLING A STARRY SKY.

THE MOMENT HE SPREAD HIS TATTERED COAT OUT TO DRY
FROM WHICH I SAW PUDDLE WATER DRIP HERE AND THERE,
I THOUGHT TO MYSELF, 'THS MAN IS FULL OF PRAYER,'
AND STARED, DEAF TO WORDS AND LOST IN MEDITATIONS,
AT HIS SACKCLOTH IN WHICH I SAW CONSTELLATIONS.

Adaptation : *Olivier Petit* - Art : *Laurent Audoin*

The Word

Face to face, in slippers,
Doors closed, at home, no witness to your whispers
You'll utter in the ear of the most mysterious
Of your heart's companions, or, if you're desirous,
All alone you'll murmur, almost silent, you know,
In a basement's deeps at some thirty feet below,
About some individual, an unkind word.
This word—which you believe that nobody has heard,
Which you whispered so low in such dark, mute places,
Flies though scarce hinted, leaves, leaps, from shadows races;
Oh, my, it's gotten out! It seems to know its way;
It has two feet, a cane in hand, it walks away,
In good, steel-toed shoes, a passport in due form;
If it needed, it would take flight on eagle's wings!
It escapes from you, nothing will stop it, it's gone;
It skirts the river's edge, crosses the square, and so on,
Boatless, passes over, in times of rain in sheets,
And proceeds right on through a labyrinth of streets,
Straight home to the citizen of whom you've spoken.
It knows his number, and his floor; the key has gotten,
It climbs up the stairs, opens the door, passes through,
Enters, walks up, and eyeballs him mockingly, too,
And says: "Straight from the lips of so and so, you see!"
So there you go. You have a mortal enemy!

People often have an image of Victor Hugo as a man with a white beard, an honorable grandfather and as someone to be studied. Right-thinking folk are all in agreement. They never lack for kind words to vaunt the importance of the poet to their children. The poet, however, found words for those old dotards which make for mortal dread.

"Oh, youth! Chosen Ones! Flowers of the living world, masters of the month of April and the rising sun, pay no heed to those people who tell you what is "good"! Good is to flee from all those dreary faces! Them, wrinkled, worn out, withered, toothless, bald, and hideous, their mournful desire flickering in their evil eyes. Oh! How I hate them, those solemn skinflints! With their gall and their disgust, they concoct a "goodness" for the elderly brewed, brimming with boredom augured and dare offer it to their brood."

From Les Contemplations, 1856.
Translation by Joe Johnson.

Adaptation : *Céka* - Art : *François Duprat*

"Tonight in clouds the sun has gone to bed..."

Tonight in clouds the sun has gone to bed.
Tomorrow, storms will come, and dusk, and night;
Then sunrise with its mist-obstructed light;
Then nights, then days—Time's ever-fleeing tread!

And all those days will pass—will pass in throngs
Across the seas and peaks and silver streams
And forests ringing with a sound that seems
Like our beloved dead chanting dim songs.

The ocean's surface, the peaks' canopy
Wrinkled but ageless, and the green woods teem
Constantly; constantly the rural stream
Draws water from the mountains to the sea.

Yet I must pass; daily my head must fall
Lower; soon, chilled beneath the sunlight's play,
During this carnival I must go away—
And the whole radiant world will lose nothing at all.

Victor Hugo
From Les Feuilles
d'Automne, 1831
Translation by E. H. and
A. M. Blackmore.

Hugo has returned from his exile. He is sixty-eight years old and has fifteen years remaining to him. He continues to write and to make love. To one mistress, who is only twenty-two years old, he writes: "We are both close to Heaven, Madame, for you are beautiful and I am old." He is elected senator. There is an endless parade of honors for him both French and foreign. His eightieth birthday is declared a national holiday, and the Avenue d'Eylau is renamed the Avenue Victor-Hugo. But resting on his many laurels he will not. If, from a distant land, he is summoned to defend the condemned, he gladly goes there. On April 5, 1885, he honors a new lady, but falls very ill soon after. During his agony, he still finds the strength to say one last verse: "Here is the struggle of day and night." It is May 22, 1885. A sun set that evening. Ever since, the firmament of writers has shone a little less brightly.

TONIGHT IN CLOUDS
THE SUN HAS GONE TO BED.

TOMORROW, STORMS WILL
COME, AND DUSK, AND NIGHT;

THEN SUNRISE WITH ITS
MIST-OBSTRUCTED LIGHT;

Bibliography

Blackmore, E. H. and A. M., trans. *Selected Poems of Victor Hugo, A Bilingual Edition.* Chicago: University of Chicago Press, 2001.

Hugo, Victor. *Poems in three volumes.* Centenary Edition. Boston: Dana Estes & Company, n.d.

Lazarus, Emma. *Poems and Translations. Written between the ages of fourteen and seventeen.* New York: Hurd & Houghton, 1867.

Williams, Henry Llewellyn, ed. and trans. *Selections Chiefly Lyrical from the Poetical Works of Victor Hugo. Translated into English by Various Authors.* London: George Bell and Sons, 1887.

ComicsLit is an imprint
and trademark of

NANTIER · BEALL · MINOUSTCHINE
Publishing inc.
new york

Vous avez les d
les deux, vibrat
gai remuent tran
et la douceur
altions en rendez
beaus que vous
gai en avez pas
Mon émotion qu
Vous direz de